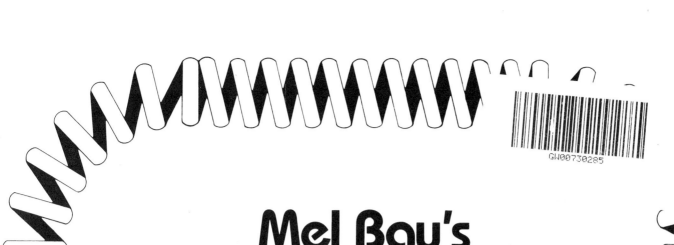

Mel Bay's
FAVORITE
ACCORDION
SOLOS

By Frank Zucco

Foreword

Mel Bay's Favorite Accordion Solos is an outstanding collection of accordion solos. The music is from various periods and represents a colorful assortment of styles. The arrangements are quite unique to the accordion. This text should provide much needed solo and recital material for any accordion performer.

Table of Contents

Page

To Mr. Grieg _____ 4

Mora Tango _____ 6

Crazy-Legs _____ 8

Adagio (Beethoven) _____ 10

Classic Medley _____ 11

    Grieg's Concerto
    Ode To Joy
    William Tell
    Tocatta/Bach
    Beethoven's Fifth
    Dance of the Comedians
    Romeo & Juliet

German Dance (Beethoven) _____ 18

Sonanbula Tango _____ 20

Tango in A Minor _____ 22

Sonatina _____ 27

Bow & Arrow Polka _____ 30

Villa Rosa _____ 32

Scherzo _____ 35

Aria _____ 37

The Rosary _____ 38

Softly Now The Light of Day _____ 39

Old Time Religion _____ 39

G Minor Symphony (#40/Mozart) _____ 40

Maple Leaf Rag _____ 42

To Mr. Grieg

F. Burgmueller

Mora Tango

F. C. Z.

Crazy - Legs

F. C. Z.

9

Adagio

From The String Quartet, Opus-59-No-1

L. Van Beethoven

Classic Medley

Grieg's Concerto

Ode to Joy

William Tell

Tocatta - Bach

Beethoven's Fifth

Dance of the Comedians

Romeo & Juliet

1. Greig Concerto A minor
2. Ode to Joy Beethoven
3. William Tell Oveture
4. Toccata and Fugue-Bach
5. Beethoven C minor Sym.
6. Comedian's Dance-Smetna
7. Romeo and Juliet

German Dance

I

Beethoven

Sonambula Tango

F. C. Z.

Tango in A Minor
Fuego

F. C. Z.

Sonatina

F. C. Z.

Bow and Arrow Polka

F. C. Z.

Fine

Fine

mf

mf

D.C. al Fine

31

Villa Rosa
Valse Espanole

F. C. Z.

Omoroso

D.C. al Fine

34

Scherzo

F. C. Z.

Aria
Piemontese

Slowly with expression

F. C. Z.

legato sempre   *mi*

The Rosary

Nevin F. C. Z.

Softly Now the Light of Day

C. M. Von Weber
F. C. Z.

Old Time Religion

Unknown
F. C. Z.

G Minor Symphony No. 40

Mozart F. C. Z.

Maple Leaf Rag

Joplin F. C. Z.

42